卞尺丹几乙し丹卞と

Translated Language Learning

The Little Mermaid

リトル・マーメイド

Hans Christian Andersen

English /日本語

Copyright © 2023 Tranzlaty
All rights reserved.
Published by Tranzlaty
ISBN: 978-1-83566-287-8
Original text by Hans Christian Andersen
Den Lille Havfrue
First published in Danish in 1837
www.tranzlaty.com

The Little Mermaid
リトル・マーメイド

Far out in the ocean, where the water is blue
海のはるか彼方、水が青いところ
here the water is as blue as the prettiest cornflower
ここでは、水は最も美しいヤグルマギクのように青いです
and the water is as clear as the purest crystal
そして、水は最も純粋な水晶のように澄んでいます
this water, far out in the ocean is very, very deep
この水は、はるか海の彼方にあり、とてもとても深いです
water so deep, indeed, that no cable could reach the bottom
実際、水深が深く、ケーブルが底に届かなかった
you could pile many church steeples upon each other
教会の尖塔をいくつも重ねることができます
but they would not reach the surface of the water
しかし、それらは水面に届きません
There dwell the Sea King and his subjects
そこには海王とその臣下が住んでいる
you might think it is just bare yellow sand at the bottom
底がむき出しの黄色い砂だと思うかもしれません
but we must not imagine that there is nothing there
しかし、そこに何もないと想像してはいけません
on this sand grow the strangest flowers and plants
この砂の上には、奇妙な花や植物が生えています
and you can't imagine how pliant the leaves and stems are
そして、葉や茎がどれほどしなやかであるかは想像もつきません
the slightest agitation of the water causes them to stir
水がわずかに撹拌されると、それらがかき混ぜられます
it is as if each leaf had a life of their own
あたかも、一枚一枚の葉に命があるかのようです
Fishes, both large and small, glide between the branches
大小の魚が枝の間を滑空します
just like when birds fly among the trees here upon land
鳥が陸地の木々の間を飛ぶときのように

In the deepest spot of all stands a beautiful castle
最も深い場所には、美しい城が立っています
this beautiful castle is the castle of the Sea King
この美しい城は海王の城です
the walls of the castle are built of coral
城の壁は珊瑚でできています
and the long Gothic windows are of the clearest amber
長いゴシック様式の窓は最も澄んだ琥珀色です
The roof of the castle is formed of sea shells
城の屋根は貝殻でできています
and the shells open and close as the water flows over them
そして、水が貝殻の上を流れると、貝殻が開いたり閉じたりします
Their appearance is more beautiful than can be described
その姿は言葉では言い表せないほど美しい
within each shell there lies a glittering pearl
それぞれの貝殻の中には、きらめく真珠が眠っています
and each pearl would be fit for the diadem of a queen
そして、それぞれの真珠は女王の王冠にふさわしいでしょう

The Sea King had been a widower for many years
海王は長年男やもめでした
and his aged mother kept house for him
年老いた母親が彼のために家を守ってくれた
She was a very sensible woman
彼女はとても賢明な女性でした
but she was exceedingly proud of her high birth
しかし、彼女は自分の高貴な生まれを非常に誇りに思っていました
and on that account she wore twelve oysters on her tail
そのために、尾に12個の牡蠣をつけました
others of high rank were only allowed to wear six oysters
他の高位の牡蠣は6個しか着ることが許されなかった
She was, however, deserving of very great praise
しかし、彼女は非常に大きな賞賛に値しました
there was something she especially deserved praise for
彼女には特に賞賛に値するものがあった

she took great care of the the little sea princesses
彼女は小さな海のお姫様をとても大切にしました
she had six granddaughters that she loved
彼女には6人の孫娘がいて、彼女も可愛がっていた
all the sea princesses were beautiful children
海のお姫様はみんな美しい子でした
but the youngest sea princess was the prettiest of them
しかし、最年少の海姫は彼らの中で最も美しかったです
Her skin was as clear and delicate as a rose leaf
彼女の肌は薔薇の葉のように透き通っていて繊細だった
and her eyes were as blue as the deepest sea
そして彼女の瞳は最も深い海のように青かった
but, like all the others, she had no feet
しかし、他の皆と同じように、彼女には足がなかった
and at the end of her body was a fish's tail
そして、彼女の体の先には魚の尾がありました

All day long they played in the great halls of the castle
一日中、城の大広間で遊んだ
out of the walls of the castle grew beautiful flowers
城壁からは美しい花が咲いていました
and she loved to play among the living flowers, too
そして、生きた花の中で遊ぶのも大好きでした
The large amber windows were open, and the fish swam in
大きな琥珀色の窓が開いていて、魚が泳いで入ってきた
it is just like when we leave the windows open
窓を開けっ放しにしておくときと同じです
and then the pretty swallows fly into our houses
そして、かわいらしいツバメが私たちの家に飛んできます
only the fishes swam up to the princesses
魚だけがお姫様のところまで泳いでいきました
they were the only ones that ate out of their hands
手から食べたのは彼らだけでした
and they allowed themselves to be stroked by them
そして、彼らは彼らに撫でられるのを許した

Outside the castle there was a beautiful garden
城の外には美しい庭園がありました
in the garden grew bright-red and dark-blue flowers
庭には鮮やかな赤や紺色の花が咲いていました
and there grew blossoms like flames of fire
そして、そこには火の炎のような花が咲いていた
the fruit on the plants glittered like gold
植物の実は金色に輝いていた
and the leaves and stems continually waved to and fro
そして、葉や茎は絶えずあちこちに揺れていました
The earth on the ground was the finest sand
地上の土は最高級の砂だった
but it does not have the colour of the sand we know
しかし、それは私たちが知っている砂の色を持っていません
it is as blue as the flame of burning sulphur
硫黄を燃やす炎のように青い
Over everything lay a peculiar blue radiance
あらゆるものの上には、独特の青い輝きが横たわっていた
it is as if the blue sky were everywhere
まるで青空がどこまでも広がっているかのようです
the blue of the sky was above and below
空の青は上と下にあった
In calm weather the sun could be seen
穏やかな天気では、太陽が見えました
from here the sun looked like a reddish-purple flower
ここから見ると、太陽は赤紫色の花のように見えました
and the light streamed from the calyx of the flower
そして、花の萼から光が流れ出た

the palace garden was divided into several parts
宮殿の庭はいくつかの部分に分かれていました
Each of the princesses had their own little plot of ground
お姫様たちはそれぞれに小さな土地を持っていました
on this plot they could plant whatever flowers they pleased
この区画には、好きな花を植えることができました
one princess arranged her flower bed in the form of a whale
あるお姫様は、花壇をクジラの形にアレンジしました

one princess arranged her flowers like a little mermaid
一人のお姫様が人魚姫のように花を生けました
and the youngest child made her garden round, like the sun
そして、一番下の子は、太陽のように庭を丸くしました
and in her garden grew beautiful red flowers
庭には美しい赤い花が咲いていました
these flowers were as red as the rays of the sunset
その花々は夕焼けのように赤かった

She was a strange child; quiet and thoughtful
彼女は不思議な子だった。静かで思慮深い
her sisters showed delight at the wonderful things
彼女の姉妹は素晴らしいことに喜びを示しました
the things they obtained from the wrecks of vessels
船の残骸から得たもの
but she cared only for her pretty red flowers
しかし、彼女は可憐な赤い花だけを気にかけていました
although there was also a beautiful marble statue
綺麗な大理石の像もありましたが
It was the representation of a handsome boy
それはハンサムな男の子の表現でした
it had been carved out of pure white stone
それは純白の石から彫り出されていた
and it had fallen to the bottom of the sea from a wreck
そして、それは難破船から海の底に落ちていました
this marble statue of a boy she cared about too
彼女が気にかけていた男の子のこの大理石の像

She planted, by the statue, a rose-colored weeping willow
彼女は像のそばに、バラ色のしだれ柳を植えました
and soon the willow hung its fresh branches over the statue
やがて柳は新しい枝を像の上に垂らしました
the branches almost reached down to the blue sands
枝は青い砂浜まで届きそうだった
The shadows of the tree had the color of violet
木の影は紫色をしていた
and the shadows waved to and fro like the branches

影は枝のようにあちこちに揺れていた
all of this created the most interesting illusion
これらすべてが、最も興味深い錯覚を生み出しました
as if the crown of the tree and the roots were playing
まるで木の冠と根っこが遊んでいるかのように
it looked as if they were trying to kiss each other
まるでキスをしようとしているかのようだった

her greatest pleasure was hearing about the world above
彼女の最大の喜びは、天上の世界について聞くことでした
the world above the deep sea she lived in
彼女が住んでいた深海の上の世界
She made her old grandmother tell her all about it
彼女は年老いた祖母にそのことをすべて話させました
the ships and the towns, the people and the animals
船と町、人々と動物
up there the flowers of the land had fragrance
そこには大地の花々が芳香を漂わせていた
the flowers below the sea had no fragrance
海の下の花には香りがなかった
up there the trees of the forest were green
そこには森の木々が緑を茂らせていた
and the fishes in the trees could sing beautifully
そして、木々の魚は美しく歌うことができました
up there it was a pleasure to listen to the fish
そこでは、魚の声を聞くのが楽しみでした
her grandmother called the birds fishes
彼女の祖母は鳥を魚と呼んでいました
else the little mermaid would not have understood
そうでなければ、人魚姫は理解できなかったでしょう
because the little mermaid had never seen birds
人魚姫は鳥を見たことがなかったからです

her grandmother told her about the rites of mermaids
彼女の祖母は彼女に人魚の儀式について話しました
"one day you will reach your fifteenth year"
「いつか15歳になる」

"then you will have permission to go to the surface"
「そうすれば、地表に出る許可が下りる」
"you will be able to sit on the rocks in the moonlight"
「月明かりに照らされた岩の上に座れるようになる」
"and you will see the great ships go sailing by"
「そして、大きな船が通り過ぎるのを見るでしょう」
"Then you will see forests and towns and the people"
「そうすれば、森や町や人々が見える」

the following year one of the sisters would be fifteen
翌年、姉妹の一人は15歳になりました
but each sister was a year younger than the other
しかし、姉妹はそれぞれ一歳年下でした
the youngest would have to wait five years before her turn
末っ子は順番が来るまで5年待たなければならなかった
only then could she rise up from the bottom of the ocean
そうして初めて、彼女は海の底から這い上がることができたのです
and only then could she see the earth as we do
そうして初めて、彼女は私たちと同じように地球を見ることができたのです
However, each of the sisters made each other a promise
しかし、姉妹はお互いに約束を交わしました
they were going to tell the others what they had seen
彼らは自分たちが見たことを他の者たちに話そうとしていた
Their grandmother could not tell them enough
彼らの祖母は彼らに十分に話すことができませんでした
there were so many things they wanted to know about
知りたいことがたくさんあった

the youngest sister longed for her turn the most
一番下の妹が自分の番を一番待ち望んでいた
but, she had to wait longer than all the others
しかし、彼女は他の誰よりも長く待たなければなりませんでした
and she was so quiet and thoughtful about the world
そして、彼女はとても静かで、世界について思慮深い人でし

た
there were many nights where she stood by the open window
開け放たれた窓辺に佇む夜も多かった
and she looked up through the dark blue water
そして彼女は紺碧の水面から顔を上げた
and she watched the fish as they splashed with their fins
そして、魚がヒレで水しぶきを上げるのを見ました
She could see the moon and stars shining faintly
月と星がかすかに輝いているのが見えた
but from deep below the water these things look different
しかし、水面下深くから見ると、これらのものは違って見えます
the moon and stars looked larger than they do to our eyes
月や星は、私たちの目には大きく見えました
sometimes, something like a black cloud went past
時折、黒い雲のようなものが通り過ぎた
she knew that it could be a whale swimming over her head
頭上を泳ぐクジラかもしれないと彼女は知っていた
or it could be a ship, full of human beings
あるいは、人間でいっぱいの船かもしれません
human beings who couldn't imagine what was under them
足元に何があるのか想像もつかない人間たち
a pretty little mermaid holding out her white hands
白い手を差し出す可憐な人魚
a pretty little mermaid reaching towards their ship
船に向かって手を伸ばす可愛らしい人魚

the day came when the eldest had her fifteenth birthday
長女が15歳の誕生日を迎える日がやってきた
now she was allowed to rise to the surface of the ocean
今、彼女は海面に浮かび上がることを許されました
and that night she swum up to the surface
そしてその夜、彼女は水面まで泳ぎ上がった
you can imagine all the things she saw up there
彼女がそこで見たすべてのものを想像することができます
and you can imagine all the things she had to talk about

そして、彼女が話さなければならなかったすべてのことを想像することができます

But the finest thing, she said, was to lie on a sand bank
しかし、一番いいのは砂の土手に横たわることだったと彼女は言った

in the quiet moonlit sea, near the shore
静かな月明かりに照らされた海で、海岸近くで

from there she had gazed at the lights on the land
そこから彼女は大地の明かりを見つめていた

they were the lights of the near-by town
それらは近くの町の明かりだった

the lights had twinkled like hundreds of stars
光は何百もの星のようにきらめいていた

she had listened to the sounds of music from the town
彼女は町の音楽の音に耳を傾けていた

she had heard noise of carriages drawn by their horses
馬が引く馬車の音が聞こえた

and she had heard the voices of human beings
そして、彼女は人間の声を聞いた

and the had heard merry pealing of the bells
そして、鐘の陽気な音を聞いた

the bells ringing in the church steeples
教会の尖塔に鳴り響く鐘

but she could not go near all these wonderful things
しかし、彼女はこれらすべての素晴らしいものに近づくことができませんでした

so she longed for these wonderful things all the more
だから、彼女はこれらの素晴らしいものをますます切望しました

you can imagine how eagerly the youngest sister listened
末の妹がどれほど熱心に耳を傾けたかは想像に難くありません

the descriptions of the upper world were like a dream
上の世界の描写は夢のようでした

afterwards she stood at the open window of her room
その後、彼女は自分の部屋の開いた窓の前に立っていた

and she looked to the surface, through the dark-blue water
そして彼女は紺色の水面から水面を見た
she thought of the great city her sister had told her of
彼女は姉が教えてくれた大都会を思い浮かべた
the great city with all its bustle and noise
喧騒と喧騒に満ちた大都会
she even fancied she could hear the sound of the bells
鐘の音が聞こえるとさえ思った
she imagined their sound carried to the depths of the sea
その音が海の底まで運ばれていくのを想像した

after another year the second sister had her birthday
さらに1年後、次女は誕生日を迎えました
she too received permission to rise to the surface
彼女もまた、地上に浮上する許可を得た
and from there she could swim about where she pleased
そしてそこから、好きなところを泳ぐことができました
She had gone to the surface just as the sun was setting
彼女は太陽が沈む頃に水面に上がった
this, she said, was the most beautiful sight of all
これは、すべての中で最も美しい光景だったと彼女は言いました
The whole sky looked like a disk of pure gold
空全体が純金の円盤のように見えた
and there were violet and rose-colored clouds
そして、紫と薔薇色の雲がありました
they were too beautiful to describe, she said
言葉では言い表せないほど美しかった、と彼女は言った
and she said how the clouds drifted across the sky
そして、雲が空を横切って漂っていると言いました
and something had flown by more swiftly than the clouds
そして、何かが雲よりも速く飛んでいった
a large flock of wild swans flew toward the setting sun
野生の白鳥の大群が夕日に向かって飛んでいった
the swans had been like a long white veil across the sea
白鳥は海の向こうに長く白いベールをかぶっているようだった

She had also tried to swim towards the sun
彼女はまた、太陽に向かって泳ごうとしました
but some distance away the sun sank into the waves
しかし、少し離れたところで太陽は波の中に沈んでいった
she saw how the rosy tints faded from the clouds
雲からバラ色の色合いが消えていくのが見えた
and she saw how the colour had also faded from the sea
そして、海から色が消えていくのが見えました

the next year it was the third sister's turn
翌年は三番目の妹の番でした
this sister was the boldest of all the sisters
この姉妹は、すべての姉妹の中で一番大胆でした
she swam up a broad river that emptied into the sea
彼女は海に注ぐ広い川を泳いで上った
On the banks of the river she saw green hills
川のほとりに緑の丘が見えた
the green hills were covered with beautiful vines
緑の丘は美しいブドウの木で覆われていました
and on the hills there were forests of trees
丘の上には木々の森がありました
and out of the forests palaces and castles poked out
森から宮殿や城が突き出ていました
She had heard birds singing in the trees
木々のさえずりで鳥のさえずりが聞こえた
and she had felt the rays of the sun on her skin
太陽の光を肌に感じた
the rays were so strong that she had to dive back
光線があまりに強かったので、彼女は飛び込まなければならなかった
and she cooled her burning face in the cool water
そして、彼女は火照った顔を冷たい水で冷やした
In a narrow creek she found a group of little children
狭い小川で、彼女は小さな子供たちのグループを見つけました
they were the first human children she had ever seen
それは彼女が初めて見た人間の子供だった

She wanted to play with the children too
子供たちと遊びたかった
but the children fled from her in a great fright
しかし、子供たちはひどく怯えて彼女から逃げ出しました
and then a little black animal came to the water
すると、小さな黒い動物が水にやって来ました
it was a dog, but she did not know it was a dog
それは犬だったが、彼女はそれが犬だとは知らなかった
because she had never seen a dog before
なぜなら、彼女はそれまで犬を見たことがなかったからです
and the dog barked at the mermaid furiously
そして犬は人魚に猛烈に吠えました
she became frightened and rushed back to the open sea
彼女は怯え、大海原へと急いで戻った
But she said she should never forget the beautiful forest
しかし、彼女は美しい森を決して忘れてはいけないと言いました
the green hills and the pretty children
緑の丘と可愛い子供たち
she found it exceptionally funny how they swam
彼女は、彼らの泳ぎ方を非常に面白いと感じました
because the little human children didn't have tails
小さな人間の子供には尻尾がなかったからです
so with their little legs they kicked the water
それで、小さな足で水を蹴りました

The fourth sister was more timid than the last
4番目の妹は、前の妹よりも臆病でした
She had decided to stay in the midst of the sea
彼女は海の真ん中にとどまることに決めていた
but she said it was as beautiful there as nearer the land
しかし、彼女は、そこは陸地に近いのと同じくらい美しいと言いました
from the surface she could see many miles around her
地表からは周囲が何マイルも見渡せた
the sky above her looked like a bell of glass
頭上の空はガラスの鐘のようだった

and she had seen the ships sail by
そして、船が通り過ぎるのを見た
but they were at a very great distance from her
しかし、彼らは彼女から非常に遠く離れていました
and, with their sails, they looked like sea gulls
そして、帆を張った姿は、まるでカモメのようでした
she saw how the dolphins played in the waves
彼女はイルカが波の中で遊ぶ様子を見ました
and great whales spouted water from their nostrils
大きなクジラは鼻の穴から水を噴き出しました
like a hundred fountains all playing together
100の噴水が一緒に遊んでいるように

The fifth sister's birthday occurred in the winter
5番目の妹の誕生日は冬に起こりました
so she saw things that the others had not seen
それで、彼女は他の人が見ていないものを見ました
at this time of the year the sea looked green
この時期は海が緑に見えました
large icebergs were floating on the green water
大きな氷山が緑の水面に浮かんでいた
and each iceberg looked like a pearl, she said
そして、それぞれの氷山は真珠のように見えた、と彼女は言った
but they were larger and loftier than the churches
しかし、それらは教会よりも大きく、高かった
and they were of the most interesting shapes
そして、それらは最も興味深い形をしていました
and each iceberg glittered like diamonds
そして、それぞれの氷山がダイヤモンドのようにきらめきました
She had seated herself on one of the Icebergs
彼女は氷山の一つに腰を下ろしていた
and she let the wind play with her long hair
そして彼女は長い髪を風に翻弄した
She noticed something interesting about the ships
彼女は船について興味深いことに気づいた

all the ships sailed past the icebergs very rapidly
すべての船は氷山を非常に速く通過しました
and they steered away as far as they could
そして、彼らはできるだけ遠くへ舵を切った
it was as if they were afraid of the iceberg
まるで氷山を恐れているかのようだった
she stayed out at sea into the evening
彼女は夕方まで海にいた
the sun went down and dark clouds covered the sky
太陽が沈み、暗い雲が空を覆った
the thunder rolled across the ocean of icebergs
雷鳴が氷山の海を横切った
and the flashes of lightning glowed red on the icebergs
そして、稲妻の閃光が氷山を赤く輝かせた
and they were tossed about by the heaving sea
そして、彼らはうねる海に翻弄された
all the ships the sails were trembling with fear
帆を張ったすべての船が恐怖に震えていた
and the mermaid sat calmly on the floating iceberg
そして人魚は浮かぶ氷山の上に静かに座っていました
she watched the lightning strike into the sea
彼女は稲妻が海に落ちるのを見た

All of her five older sisters had grown up now
5人の姉たちは皆、大人になっていた
therefore they could go to the surface when they pleased
それゆえ、彼らは好きなときに水面に出ることができたのです
at first they were delighted with the surface world
最初、彼らは地上の世界に喜んでいました
they couldn't get enough of the new and beautiful sights
彼らは新しくて美しい光景に飽き足らなかった
but eventually they all grew indifferent towards it
しかし、やがて彼らは皆、それに対して無関心になっていった
and after a month they didn't visit much at all anymore
そして、一ヶ月後、彼らはもうあまり訪れなくなりました

they told their sister it was much more beautiful at home
彼らは妹に、家の方がずっと美しいと言いました

Yet often, in the evening hours, they did go up
しかし、夕方になると、彼らはしばしば上がった
the five sisters twined their arms about each other
五姉妹はお互いに腕を絡め合った
and together, arm in arm, they rose to the surface
そして一緒に、腕を組んで、彼らは水面に浮かび上がった
often they went up when there was a storm approaching
嵐が近づいてくると、よく上がった
they feared that the storm might win a ship
彼らは、嵐が船を奪うかもしれないと恐れた
so they swam to the vessel and sung to the sailors
それで彼らは船まで泳ぎ、船員たちに歌いました
Their voices were more charming than that of any human
その声は、人間の声よりも魅力的だった
and they begged the voyagers not to fear if they sank
そして、彼らは航海者たちに、沈んでも恐れないでくれと懇願した
because the depths of the sea was full of delights
深海は喜びに満ちていたからです
But the sailors could not understand their songs
しかし、船乗りたちは彼らの歌を理解することができませんでした
and they thought their singing was the sighing of the storm
そして、彼らは自分たちの歌を嵐のため息だと思った
therefore their songs were never beautiful to the sailors
それゆえ、彼らの歌は船乗りたちにとって決して美しいものではなかった
because if the ship sank the men would drown
船が沈めば、男たちは溺れてしまうからだ
the dead gained nothing from the palace of the Sea King
死者は海王の宮殿から何も得られなかった
but their youngest sister was left at the bottom of the sea
しかし、一番下の妹は海の底に置き去りにされました
looking up at them, she was ready to cry

二人を見上げて、彼女は今にも泣き出しそうだった
you should know mermaids have no tears that they can cry
人魚には泣ける涙がないことを知っておく必要があります
so her pain and suffering was more acute than ours
ですから、彼女の痛みと苦しみは私たちよりも深刻でした
"Oh, I wish I was also fifteen years old!" said she
「ああ、私も15歳だったらよかったのに!」と彼女は言いました
"I know that I shall love the world up there"
「私はあそこの世界を愛することを知っています」
"and I shall love all the people who live in that world"
「そして、私はその世界に住むすべての人々を愛するでしょう」

but, at last, she too reached her fifteenth year
しかし、ついに彼女も15歳を迎えました
"Well, now you are grown up," said her grandmother
「まあ、もう大人になったわね」とおばあさんが言いました
"Come, and let me adorn you like your sisters"
「さあ、お姉さんたちのように飾りましょう」
And she placed a wreath of white lilies in her hair
そして、白い百合の花輪を髪につけました
every petal of the lilies was half a pearl
ユリの花びらは一枚一枚、真珠の半分だった
Then, the old lady ordered eight great oysters to come
すると、おばあさんは大きな牡蠣を8個持ってくるように命じました
the oysters attached themselves to the tail of the princess
牡蠣はお姫様の尻尾にくっつきました
under the sea oysters are used to show your rank
海底牡蠣はランクを示すために使用されます
"But they hurt me so," said the little mermaid
「でも、あいつらはあたしをひどく傷つけたのよ」と人魚姫は言いました
"Yes, I know oysters hurt," replied the old lady
「ええ、牡蠣が痛いのは知っています」とおばあさんは答えました

"but you know very well that pride must suffer pain"
「しかし、プライドは痛みを伴わなければならないことを、あなたはよく知っています」
how gladly she would have shaken off all this grandeur
この壮大さを振り払ったことがどれほど嬉しかったことか
she would have loved to lay aside the heavy wreath!
彼女は重い花輪を脇に置いておくのが大好きだったでしょう!
she thought of the red flowers in her own garden
彼女は自分の庭の赤い花を思い浮かべた
the red flowers would have suited her much better
赤い花の方がずっと似合っていただろう
But she could not change herself into something else
しかし、彼女は自分を他の何かに変えることはできなかった
so she said farewell to her grandmother and sisters
それで、彼女は祖母と姉妹に別れを告げました
and, as lightly as a bubble, she rose to the surface
そして、泡のように軽やかに、彼女は水面に浮かび上がった

The sun had just set when she raised her head above the waves
彼女が波の上に顔を上げた時、太陽はちょうど沈んだところだった
The clouds were tinted with crimson and gold from the sunset
雲は夕焼けで深紅と金色に染まっていました
and through the glimmering twilight beamed the evening star
そして、きらめく黄昏を通して宵の明星を照らしました
The sea was calm, and the sea air was mild and fresh
海は穏やかで、海の空気は穏やかで新鮮でした
A large ship with three masts lay becalmed on the water
3本のマストを持つ大きな船が水面に横たわっていた
only one sail was set, for not a breeze stirred
帆は一枚だけ張られ、そよ風は一本も揺れなかった
and the sailors sat idle on deck, or amidst the rigging
そして、水兵たちは甲板で、あるいは艤装の真ん中でぼんやりと座っていた

There was music and song on board of the ship
船内には音楽と歌がありました
as darkness came a hundred colored lanterns were lighted
暗闇が訪れると、100個の色とりどりのランタンが灯されました
it was as if the flags of all nations waved in the air
あたかもすべての国の国旗が宙に振られているかのようでした

The little mermaid swam close to the cabin windows
人魚姫は小屋の窓の近くを泳ぎました
now and then the waves of the sea lifted her up
時折、海の波が彼女を持ち上げた
she could look in through the glass window-panes
彼女はガラス窓ガラス越しに中を覗くことができた
and she could see a number of curiously dressed people
そして、不思議な服装をした人たちが何人も見えました
Among the people she could see there was a young prince
彼女が見たのは、若い王子様の姿でした
the prince was the most beautiful of them all
王子様は、その中で一番美しかったです
she had never seen anyone with such beautiful eyes
あんなに綺麗な瞳の人は見たことがなかった
it was the celebration of his sixteenth birthday
それは彼の16歳の誕生日のお祝いでした
The sailors were dancing on the deck of the ship
船員たちは船の甲板で踊っていた
all cheered when the prince came out of the cabin
王子が小屋から出てくると、みんなが歓声を上げた
and more than a hundred rockets rose into the air
そして100発以上のロケット弾が空中に舞い上がった
for some time the fireworks made the sky as bright as day
しばらくの間、花火は空を昼のように明るくしました
of course our young mermaid had never seen fireworks before
もちろん、私たちの若い人魚は花火を見たことがありませんでした

startled by all the noise, she dived back under water
その音に驚いて、彼女は水中に潜った
but soon she again stretched out her head
しかしすぐに、彼女は再び頭を伸ばした
it was as if all the stars of heaven were falling around her
まるで天の星々が彼女の周りに降り注いでいるかのようでした
splendid fireflies flew up into the blue air
見事なホタルが青い空に舞い上がりました
and everything was reflected in the clear, calm sea
そして、すべてが澄んだ穏やかな海に反映されました
The ship itself was brightly illuminated by all the light
船自体がすべての光で明るく照らされていました
she could see all the people and even the smallest rope
彼女はすべての人々を見ることができ、最も小さなロープさえも見ることができました
How handsome the young prince looked thanking his guests!
若い王子は、ゲストにお礼を言うなんて、なんとハンサムな姿だったのでしょう。
and the music resounded through the clear night air!
そして、澄んだ夜の空気に音楽が響き渡りました！

the birthday celebrations lasted late into the night
誕生日のお祝いは夜遅くまで続きました
but the little mermaid could not take her eyes from the ship
しかし、人魚姫は船から目を離すことができませんでした
nor could she take her eyes from the beautiful prince
美しい王子から目を離すこともできなかった
The colored lanterns had now been extinguished
色とりどりの提灯は消えていた
and there were no more rockets that rose into the air
そして、空中に舞い上がったロケットはもうありませんでした
the cannon of the ship had also ceased firing
船の大砲も発射をやめていた
but now it was the sea that became restless

しかし、今、落ち着きを失ったのは海でした
a moaning, grumbling sound could be heard beneath the waves
うめき声、うめき声、うめき声が波の下に聞こえた
and yet, the little mermaid remained by the cabin window
それなのに、人魚姫は船室の窓のそばにいました
she was rocking up and down on the water
彼女は水面を上下に揺れていた
so that she could keep looking into the ship
船の中を覗き込み続けられるように
After a while the sails were quickly set
しばらくすると、すぐに帆が張られました
and the ship went on her way back to port
そして船は港に帰って行きました

But soon the waves rose higher and higher
しかし、すぐに波はどんどん高くなっていきました
dark, heavy clouds darkened the night sky
暗く重い雲が夜空を暗くした
and there appeared flashes of lightning in the distance
すると、遠くに稲妻の閃光が現れました
not far away a dreadful storm was approaching
そう遠くないところで、恐ろしい嵐が近づいていました
Once more the sails were lowered against the wind
もう一度、帆が風に逆らって降ろされた
and the great ship pursued her course over the raging sea
そして、大きな船は荒れ狂う海の上を進路をとった
The waves rose as high as the mountains
波は山のように高く上がった
one would have thought the waves would have had the ship
波が船を持っていただろうと思ったでしょう
but the ship dived like a swan between the waves
しかし、船は波の間を白鳥のように潜った
then she rose again on their lofty, foaming crests
そして彼女は再び、その高く泡立つ頂上に立ち上がった
To the little mermaid this was pleasant sport
人魚姫にとって、これは楽しいスポーツでした

but it was not pleasant sport to the sailors
しかし、それは船員にとって楽しいスポーツではありませんでした
the ship made awful groaning and creaking sounds
船はひどいうめき声と軋む音を立てた
and the waves broke over the deck again and again
そして、波は何度も何度も甲板を打ち砕きました
the thick planks gave way under the lashing of the sea
厚い板は海の打ち付けに屈した
under the pressure the mainmast snapped asunder, like a reed
その圧力でメインマストは葦のように折れた
and, as the ship lay over on her side, the water rushed in
そして、船が横倒しになると、水が押し寄せてきました

The little mermaid realized that the crew were in danger
人魚姫は乗組員が危険にさらされていることに気づきました
her own situation wasn't without danger either
彼女自身の状況にも危険がなかったわけではない
she had to avoid the beams and planks scattered in the water
彼女は水中に散らばった梁や板を避けなければならなかった
for a moment everything turned into complete darkness
一瞬、すべてが真っ暗闇に変わりました
and the little mermaid could not see where she was
人魚姆は自分がどこにいるのかわかりませんでした
but then a flash of lightning revealed the whole scene
しかし、その時、稲妻の閃光がシーンの一部始終を露わにした
she could see everyone was still on board of the ship
全員がまだ船に乗っているのが見えた
well, everyone was on board of the ship, except the prince
まあ、王子様以外はみんな船に乗っていました
the ship continued on its path to the land
船は陸地への道を歩み続けた
and she saw the prince sink into the deep waves
そして、王子が深い波に沈んでいくのが見えました
for a moment this made her happier than it should have

一瞬、これは彼女を必要以上に幸せにした
now that he was in the sea she could be with him
彼が海にいた今、彼女は彼と一緒にいることができました
Then she remembered the limits of human beings
そして、人間の限界を思い出した
the people of the land cannot live in the water
土地の人々は水の中で暮らすことはできません
if he got to the palace he would already be dead
宮殿にたどり着いたら、とっくに死んでいる
"No, he must not die!" she decided
「いや、死んではいけない!」と彼女は決心した
she forget any concern for her own safety
彼女は自分の安全を心配することを忘れている
and she swam through the beams and planks
そして、梁や板の間を泳ぎました
two beams could easily crush her to pieces
二本の梁で彼女を粉々に砕き散らす
she dove deep under the dark waters
彼女は暗い海の奥深くに潜った
everything rose and fell with the waves
すべてが波とともに上がったり下がったり
finally, she managed to reach the young prince
ようやく、彼女は若い王子にたどり着くことができました
he was fast losing the power to swim in the stormy sea
彼は嵐の海で泳ぐ力を急速に失っていました
His limbs were starting to fail him
彼の手足は彼を衰えさせ始めていた
and his beautiful eyes were closed
そして彼の美しい目は閉じられていた
he would have died had the little mermaid not come
人魚姆が来なかったら、彼は死んでいたでしょう
She held his head above the water
彼女は彼の頭を水面上にかざした
and let the waves carry them where they wanted
そして、波が彼らを望むところに運ばせてください

In the morning the storm had ceased
朝には嵐は止んでいた
but of the ship not a single fragment could be seen
しかし、船の破片は一つも見えませんでした
The sun came up, red and shining, out of the water
太陽が赤く輝いて水面から昇ってきた
the sun's beams had a healing effect on the prince
太陽の光は王子に癒しの効果をもたらしました
the hue of health returned to the prince's cheeks
王子の頬に健康の色が戻った
but despite the sun, his eyes remained closed
しかし、太陽にもかかわらず、彼の目は閉じたままでした
The mermaid kissed his high, smooth forehead
人魚は彼の高くて滑らかな額にキスをした
and she stroked back his wet hair
そして彼女は彼の濡れた髪を撫でた
He seemed to her like the marble statue in her garden
彼は庭にある大理石の彫像のように思えた
so she kissed him again, and wished that he lived
それで娘はもう一度彼にキスをして、彼が生きていたらいいのにと願った

Presently, they came in sight of land
やがて、陸地が見えてきた
and she saw lofty blue mountains on the horizon
そして、地平線上にそびえ立つ青い山々が見えた
on top of the mountains the white snow rested
山の頂上には白い雪が積もっていた
as if a flock of swans were lying upon them
まるで白鳥の群れが横たわっているかのようだ
Beautiful green forests were near the shore
海岸近くには美しい緑の森が広がっていました
and close by there stood a large building
そして、その近くには大きな建物が建っていました
it could have been a church or a convent
それは教会や修道院だったかもしれません
but she was still too far away to be sure

だが、彼女はまだ遠く離れていて、確かめることができなかった
Orange and citron trees grew in the garden
庭にはオレンジや柚子の木が生えていました
and before the door stood lofty palms
そして扉の前には、高い手のひらが立っていた
The sea here formed a little bay
ここの海は小さな湾を形成していました
in the bay the water lay quiet and still
湾の中では、水は静かで静かで横たわっていました
but although the water was still, it was very deep
しかし、水は静かでしたが、とても深かったです
She swam with the handsome prince to the beach
彼女はハンサムな王子と一緒にビーチまで泳ぎました
the beach was covered with fine white sand
浜辺は白い砂浜で覆われていた
and there she laid him in the warm sunshine
そして、彼女は彼を暖かい日差しの中に横たえました
she took care to raise his head higher than his body
彼女は彼の頭を体よりも高く上げるように注意した
Then bells sounded in the large white building
その時、大きな白い建物に鐘が鳴り響いた
some young girls came into the garden
何人かの若い女の子が庭に入ってきました
The little mermaid swam out farther from the shore
人魚姫は岸から遠くまで泳いでいきました
she hid herself among some high rocks in the water
彼女は水中の高い岩の間に身を隠しました
she Covered her head and neck with the foam of the sea
彼女は海の泡で頭と首を覆った
and she watched to see what would become of the poor prince
そして、かわいそうな王子がどうなるか見守っていました

It was not long before she saw a young girl approach
少女が近づいてくるのが見えたのは、それから間もなくだった

the young girl seemed frightened, at first
少女は最初、怯えているように見えた
but her fear only lasted for a moment
だが、彼女の恐怖は一瞬しか続かなかった
then she brought over a number of people
それから彼女は何人かの人々を連れて来ました
and the mermaid saw that the prince came to life again
そして人魚は王子が生き返ったのを見ました
he smiled upon those who stood around him
彼は周囲に立っている人々に微笑みかけた
But to the little mermaid the prince sent no smile
しかし、人魚姫に王子は微笑みを向けませんでした
he knew not that she had saved him
彼は彼女が自分を救ったことを知らなかった
This made the little mermaid very sorrowful
これは人魚姫をとても悲しませました
and then he was led away into the great building
そして、大きな建物に連れて行かれました
and the little mermaid dived down into the water
そして人魚姫は水に飛び込みました
and she returned to her father's castle
そして、彼女は父の城に戻りました

She had always been the most silent and thoughtful
彼女はいつも一番寡黙で思慮深い人だった
and now she was more silent and thoughtful than ever
そして今、彼女はかつてないほど静かで思慮深くなっていた
Her sisters asked her what she had seen on her first visit
彼女の姉妹は、彼女が最初の訪問で何を見たのか尋ねました
but she could tell them nothing of what she had seen
しかし、彼女は自分が見たことについて何も話すことができませんでした
Many an evening and morning she returned to the surface
夕方から朝にかけて、彼女は水面に戻った
and she went to the place where she had left the prince
そして、王子を置いていった場所に行きました
She saw the fruits in the garden ripen

彼女は庭の果物が熟すのを見た
and she watched the fruits gathered from their trees
そして、木から集められた果実を見ました
she watched the snow on the mountain tops melt away
山頂の雪が溶けていくのを見つめていた
but on none of her visits did she see the prince again
しかし、どの訪問でも王子に再び会うことはありませんでした
and therefore she always returned more sorrowful than before
それで、娘はいつも前よりも悲しそうに帰って来ました

her only comfort was sitting in her own little garden
彼女の唯一の慰めは、自分の小さな庭に座っていることでした
she flung her arms around the beautiful marble statue
彼女は美しい大理石の彫像に腕を回した
the statue which looked just like the prince
王子様にそっくりな像
She had given up tending to her flowers
彼女は花の世話をするのをあきらめていた
and her garden grew in wild confusion
そして彼女の庭は荒れ狂った混乱の中で成長した
they twinied their long leaves and stems round the trees
長い葉と茎を木に巻き付けました
so that the whole garden became dark and gloomy
それで、庭全体が暗く陰鬱になりました

eventually she could bear it no longer
やがて彼女は耐えられなくなった
and she told one of her sisters all about it
そして、彼女は姉妹の一人にそのことをすべて話しました
soon the other sisters heard the secret
やがて他の姉妹たちはその秘密を聞きました
and very soon her secret became known to several maids
そしてすぐに彼女の秘密は何人かのメイドに知られるようになりました

one of the maids had a friend who knew about the prince
侍女の一人に、王子のことを知っている友人がいました
She had also seen the festival on board the ship
彼女はまた、船上で祭りを見ていた
and she told them where the prince came from
そして、王子がどこから来たのか教えました
and she told them where his palace stood
そして、王女は自分の宮殿がどこにあるかを彼らに告げた

"Come, little sister," said the other princesses
「さあ、お姉ちゃん」と他のお姫様たちは言いました
they entwined their arms and rose up together
二人は腕を絡め、一緒に立ち上がった
they went near to where the prince's palace stood
二人は王子の宮殿が建っている場所に近づきました
the palace was built of bright-yellow, shining stone
宮殿は明るい黄色の輝く石で建てられました
and the palace had long flights of marble steps
宮殿には大理石の階段が長く続いていました
one of the flights of steps reached down to the sea
階段の1つは海に降りて行きました
Splendid gilded cupolas rose over the roof
華麗な金箔を貼ったキューポラが屋根の上にそびえ立っていました
the whole building was surrounded by pillars
建物全体が柱で囲まれていました
and between the pillars stood lifelike statues of marble
柱の間には、生き生きとした大理石の彫像が立っていました
they could see through the clear crystal of the windows
窓の澄んだ水晶から透けて見えた
and they could look into the noble rooms
そして、彼らは高貴な部屋を覗くことができました
costly silk curtains and tapestries hung from the ceiling
高価な絹のカーテンと天井から吊るされたタペストリー
and the walls were covered with beautiful paintings
そして壁は美しい絵で覆われていました
In the centre of the largest salon was a fountain

一番大きなサロンの中央には噴水がありました
the fountain threw its sparkling jets high up
噴水はきらめく噴流を高く投げ上げた
the water splashed onto the glass cupola of the ceiling
天井のガラスのキューポラに水しぶきがかかりました
and the sun shone in through the water
そして、太陽が水面から差し込んでいた
and the water splashed on the plants around the fountain
そして、噴水の周りの植物に水が飛び散りました

Now the little mermaid knew where the prince lived
さて、人魚姫は王子がどこに住んでいるかを知っていました
so she spent many a night on those waters
それで、彼女はその海で多くの夜を過ごしました
she got more courageous than her sisters had been
彼女は姉妹よりも勇気を出しました
and she swam much nearer the shore than they had
そして、娘は二人よりもずっと岸近くまで泳ぎました
once she went up the narrow channel, under the marble balcony
ある時、彼女は大理石のバルコニーの下、狭い水路を上った
the balcony threw a broad shadow on the water
バルコニーは水面に広い影を投げかけた
Here she sat and watched the young prince
彼女はここに座って、若い王子を見つめていました
he, of course, thought he was alone in the bright moonlight
もちろん、彼は明るい月明かりの中に一人でいると思っていました

She often saw him evenings, sailing in a beautiful boat
彼女はしばしば彼が美しいボートで航海している夜を見かけました
music sounded from the boat and the flags waved
船から音楽が鳴り響き、旗が振られた
She peeped out from among the green rushes
彼女は緑のイグサの間から顔を覗かせた
at times the wind caught her long silvery-white veil

時折、風が彼女の長い銀白色のベールを捕らえた
those who saw it believed it to be a swan
それを見た人々は、それが白鳥であると信じました
it had all the appearance of a swan spreading its wings
それは白鳥が翼を広げたような姿をしていた

Many a night, too, she watched the fishermen set their nets
また、一晩中、漁師たちが網を張るのを眺めていた
they cast their nets in the light of their torches
彼らは松明の光で網を投げた
and she heard them tell many good things about the prince
そして、王子のことをたくさん話すのを聞きました
this made her glad that she had saved his life
これは彼女が彼の命を救ったことを嬉しく思いました
when he was tossed around half dead on the waves
彼は波の上に半分死んでいる周りに放り出されたとき
She remembered how his head had rested on her bosom
彼女は彼の頭が自分の胸に乗せられていたことを思い出した
and she remembered how heartily she had kissed him
そして、彼女は彼に心からキスをしたことを思い出しました
but he knew nothing of all that had happened
しかし、かれは、起こったことのすべてについて何も知らなかった
the young prince could not even dream of the little mermaid
若い王子は人魚姫の夢を見ることさえできませんでした

She grew to like human beings more and more
どんどん人間を好きになっていった
she wished more and more to be able to wander their world
彼女はますます彼らの世界をさまようことができるようになりたいと願った
their world seemed to be so much larger than her own
彼らの世界は、彼女自身の世界よりもずっと広いように思えた
They could fly over the sea in ships
彼らは船で海の上を飛ぶことができました
and they could mount the high hills far above the clouds

そして、雲のはるか上の高い丘に登ることができた
in their lands they possessed woods and fields
彼らの土地には森と野原があった
the greenery stretched beyond the reach of her sight
視界の届かないところに緑が広がっていた
There was so much that she wished to know!
彼女が知りたいことはたくさんありました!
but her sisters were unable to answer all her questions
しかし、彼女の姉妹は彼女の質問にすべて答えることができませんでした
She then went to her old grandmother for answers
その後、彼女は年老いた祖母のところへ答えを求めました
her grandmother knew all about the upper world
彼女の祖母は上界のことをよく知っていた
she rightly called this world "the lands above the sea"
彼女はこの世界を「海の上の国」と呼んでいました

"If human beings are not drowned, can they live forever?"
「人間は溺れなければ、永遠に生きられるのか?」
"Do they never die, as we do here in the sea?"
「海でやっているように、死なないの?」
"Yes, they die too" replied the old lady
「ええ、彼らも死にます」とおばあさんは答えました
"like us, they must also die," added her grandmother
「私たちと同じように、彼らも死ななければならない」と祖母は付け加えた
"and their lives are even shorter than ours"
「そして、彼らの人生は私たちの人生よりもさらに短いのです」
"We sometimes live for three hundred years"
「300年生きることもある」
"but when we cease to exist here we become foam"
「しかし、私たちがここで存在しなくなるとき、私たちは泡になります」
"and we float on the surface of the water"
「そして私たちは水面に浮かぶ」
"we do not have graves for those we love"

"and we have not immortal souls"
「そして、私たちには不滅の魂はありません」
"after we die we shall never live again"
「死んだら二度と生きられない」
"like the green seaweed, once it has been cut off"
「緑の海苔のように、一度切り落とされたら」
"after we die, we can never flourish more"
「死んだら、これ以上栄えることはできない」
"Human beings, on the contrary, have souls"
「逆に人間には魂がある」
"even after they're dead their souls live forever"
「死んでも魂は永遠に生きる」
"when we die our bodies turn to foam"
「死ぬと体は泡になる」
"when they die their bodies turn to dust"
「死ぬと体は塵になる」
"when we die we rise through the clear, blue water"
「死ぬとき、私たちは澄んだ青い水の中を這い上がる」
"when they die they rise up through the clear, pure air"
「死ぬとき、澄んだ澄んだ空気の中をよみがえる」
"when we die we float no further than the surface"
「死ぬとき、私たちは水面より遠くに浮かびません」
"but when they die they go beyond the glittering stars"
しかし、彼らが死ぬとき、彼らはきらめく星の彼方に行く
"we rise out of the water to the surface"
「私たちは水面から浮かび上がる」
"and we behold all the land of the earth"
「わたしたちは地のすべての地を見よ」
"they rise to unknown and glorious regions"
「彼らは未知で輝かしい領域に昇る」
"glorious and unknown regions which we shall never see"
「決して見ることのできない輝かしい未知の領域」
the little mermaid mourned her lack of a soul
人魚姫は魂のなさを嘆いた
"Why have not we immortal souls?" asked the little mermaid
「どうして不滅の魂がないの?」と人魚姫は尋ねました

"I would gladly give all the hundreds of years that I have"
「何百年もの年月を喜んで捧げます」
"I would trade it all to be a human being for one day"
「1日だけ人間になるために、すべてと引き換えにしたい」
"to have the hope of knowing such happiness"
「そんな幸せを知りたいという希望を持つこと」
"the happiness of that glorious world above the stars"
「星の上の輝かしい世界の幸せ」
"You must not think that," said the old woman
「そんなこと考えちゃいけないよ」と老婆は言いました
"We believe that we are much happier than the humans"
「私たちは人間よりもはるかに幸せだと信じています」
"and we believe we are much better off than human beings"
「そして、私たちは人間よりもはるかに良い生活をしていると信じています」

"So I shall die," said the little mermaid
「じゃあ、ぼくは死ぬんだ」と人魚姫は言いました
"being the foam of the sea, I shall be washed about"
「海の泡となって、わたしは洗われる」
"never again will I hear the music of the waves"
「もう二度と波の音楽は聞かない」
"never again will I see the pretty flowers"
「もう二度と綺麗な花は見られない」
"nor will I ever again see the red sun"
「もう二度と赤い太陽を見ることもない」
"Is there anything I can do to win an immortal soul?"
「不滅の魂を手に入れるために、私にできることはありますか?」
"No," said the old woman, "unless..."
「いや」と老婆は言った。
"there is just one way to gain a soul"
「魂を得る方法は一つしかない」
"a man has to love you more than he loves his father and mother"
男は父と母を愛する以上にあなたを愛さなければならない
"all his thoughts and love must be fixed upon you"

「彼のすべての思いと愛はあなたに固定されなければなりません」

"he has to promise to be true to you here and hereafter"
「彼は今ここでも来世もあなたに忠実であることを約束しなければなりません」

"the priest has to place his right hand in yours"
「僧侶は右手をあなたの手の中に置かなければならない」

"then your man's soul would glide into your body"
「そうすれば、あなたの男の魂があなたの体に滑り込むでしょう」

"you would get a share in the future happiness of mankind"
「人類の未来の幸福の分け前をもらう」

"He would give to you a soul and retain his own as well"
「彼はあなたに魂を与え、彼自身の魂も保持するでしょう」

"but it is impossible for this to ever happen"
「しかし、そんなことはあり得ない」

"Your fish's tail, among us, is considered beautiful"
「あなたの魚の尻尾は、私たちの間では美しいと思われています」

"but on earth your fish's tail is considered ugly"
「しかし、地球上では、あなたの魚の尻尾は醜いと見なされています」

"The humans do not know any better"
「人間はそれ以上のことを知らない」

"their standard of beauty is having two stout props"
「彼らの美しさの基準は、2つの頑丈な小道具を持っていることです」

"these two stout props they call their legs"
「この2つの頑丈な小道具は、彼らが脚と呼んでいます」

The little mermaid sighed at what appeared to be her destiny
人魚姫は自分の運命にため息をついた

and she looked sorrowfully at her fish's tail
そして悲しそうに魚の尻尾を見つめました

"Let us be happy with what we have," said the old lady
「今あるもので幸せになろう」とおばあさんは言いました

"let us dart and spring about for the three hundred years"

「300年の間、飛び回って春を飛ぼう」
"and three hundred years really is quite long enough"
「300年という年月は、実に長い」
"After that we can rest ourselves all the better"
「その後はもっと休めます」
"This evening we are going to have a court ball"
「今晩はコートボールをやるんだ」

It was one of those splendid sights we can never see on earth
それは、地球上では決して見ることのできない素晴らしい光景の一つでした
the court ball took place in a large ballroom
コートボールは大きなボールルームで行われました
The walls and the ceiling were of thick transparent crystal
壁と天井は分厚い透明なクリスタルでできていました
Many hundreds of colossal shells stood in rows on each side
何百個もの巨大な貝殻が両側に並んでいた
some were deep red, others were grass green
真っ赤なものもあれば、草の緑色もあります
and each of the shells had a blue fire in it
そして、それぞれの貝殻には青い炎が燃えていました
These lighted up the whole salon and the dancers
サロン全体とダンサーを照らしました
and the shells shone out through the walls
そして、砲弾が壁を突き破って輝いていた
so that the sea was also illuminated by their light
海もその光に照らされた
Innumerable fishes, great and small, swam past
大小無数の魚が泳いで通り過ぎた
some of their scales glowed with a purple brilliance
鱗の中には紫色の輝きを放つものもあった
and other fishes shone like silver and gold
他の魚は銀や金のように輝いていた
Through the halls flowed a broad stream
廊下には広い小川が流れていた
and in the stream danced the mermen and the mermaids
そして小川の中で半魚人と人魚が踊りました

they danced to the music of their own sweet singing
彼らは自分たちの甘い歌の音楽に合わせて踊った

No one on earth has such lovely voices as they
地球上にこれほど素敵な声の人はいません
but the little mermaid sang more sweetly than all
しかし、人魚姫は誰よりも甘く歌いました
The whole court applauded her with hands and tails
宮廷中が手と尻尾で彼女に拍手を送った
and for a moment her heart felt quite happy
そして一瞬、彼女の心はとても幸せに感じました
because she knew she had the sweetest voice in the sea
なぜなら、彼女は自分が海で一番甘い声を持っていることを知っていたからだ
and she knew she had the sweetest voice on land
そして、彼女は自分が陸で一番甘い声を持っていることを知っていました
But soon she thought again of the world above her
しかしすぐに、彼女は再び頭上の世界のことを考えた
she could not forget the charming prince
彼女は魅力的な王子を忘れることができませんでした
it reminded her that he had an immortal soul
それは彼に不滅の魂があることを思い出させた
and she could not forget that she had no immortal soul
そして、自分には不滅の魂がないことを忘れることができなかった
She crept away silently out of her father's palace
彼女は静かに父の宮殿から這い出た
everything within was full of gladness and song
中にあるものはすべて喜びと歌に満ちていた
but she sat in her own little garden, sorrowful and alone
しかし、彼女は自分の小さな庭に座って、悲しみに暮れていました
Then she heard the bugle sounding through the water
その時、ラッパの音が水面に響くのが聞こえた
and she thought, "He is certainly sailing above"
そして、彼女は「彼は確かに上を航行している」と思いまし

た
"he, the beautiful prince, in whom my wishes centre"
「彼、私の願いの中心にある美しい王子様」
"he, in whose hands I should like to place my happiness"
「あの人、私の幸せを誰の手に委ねたいのか」
"I will venture all for him, and to win an immortal soul"
「私は彼のために、そして不滅の魂を勝ち取るために、すべてを賭けます」
"my sisters are dancing in my father's palace"
「姉たちは父の宮殿で踊っている」
"but I will go to the sea witch"
「でも、海の魔女のところへ行っちゃう」
"the sea witch of whom I have always been so afraid"
「私がいつも恐れていた海の魔女」
"but the sea witch can give me counsel, and help"
「しかし、海の魔女は私に助言を与え、助けることができます」

Then the little mermaid went out from her garden
それから人魚姫は庭から出て行きました
and she took the road to the foaming whirlpools
そして彼女は泡立つ渦潮への道を進んだ
behind the foaming whirlpools the sorceress lived
泡立つ渦の向こうに魔術師が住んでいた
the little mermaid had never gone that way before
人魚姆姫はこれまでそのような道を歩んだことがありませんでした
Neither flowers nor grass grew where she was going
彼女が行くところには花も草も生えていなかった
there was nothing but bare, gray, sandy ground
そこにあるのは、むき出しの灰色の砂地だけだった
this barren land stretched out to the whirlpool
この不毛の地は渦潮まで広がっていた
the water was like foaming mill wheels
水は泡立つ水車小屋のようでした
and the mills seized everything that came within reach
そして、水車小屋は手の届くところにあるものすべてを押収

しました
they cast their prey into the fathomless deep
彼らは獲物を底知れぬ深淵に投げ込む
Through these crushing whirlpools she had to pass
この押しつぶすような渦の中を、彼女は通り抜けなければならなかった
only then could she reach the dominions of the sea witch
そうして初めて、彼女は海の魔女の領地にたどり着くことができた
after this came a stretch of warm, bubbling mire
この後、暖かく泡立つ泥沼が続きました
the sea witch called the bubbling mire her turf moor
海の魔女は泡立つ泥沼を縄張りの荒野と呼んだ

Beyond her turf moor was the witch's house
縄張りの荒野の向こうには魔女の家があった
her house stood in the centre of a strange forest
彼女の家は見知らぬ森の真ん中に立っていた
in this forest all the trees and flowers were polypi
この森では、すべての木や花がポリープでした
but they were only half plant; the other half was animal
しかし、それらは半分の植物にすぎませんでした。残りの半分は動物でした
They looked like serpents with a hundred heads
彼らは100の頭を持つ蛇のように見えました
and each serpent was growing out of the ground
そして、それぞれの蛇が地から生えていた
Their branches were long, slimy arms
その枝は長くてぬるぬるした腕だった
and they had fingers like flexible worms
そして、しなやかなミミズのような指を持っていました
each of their limbs, from the root to the top, moved
それぞれの手足が、根元から上まで動いた
All that could be reached in the sea they seized upon
彼らが掌握した海で到達できるすべてのもの
and what they caught they held on tightly to
そして、彼らが捕まえたものはしっかりと握りしめていまし

た
so that it never escaped from their clutches
それが彼らの手から逃れることがないように

The little mermaid was alarmed at what she saw
人魚姫は自分が見たものに驚愕しました
she stood still and her heart beat with fear
彼女は立ち止まり、恐怖で心臓が鼓動した
She came very close to turning back
彼女は引き返すところまで来ました
but she thought of the beautiful prince
しかし、彼女は美しい王子のことを思いました
and the thought of the human soul for which she longed
そして、彼女が憧れていた人間の魂の思い
with these thoughts her courage returned
そう思うと、勇気が戻ってきた
She fastened her long, flowing hair round her head
彼女は流れるような長い髪を頭に巻きつけた
so that the polypi could not grab hold of her hair
ポリープが彼女の髪をつかむことができないように
and she crossed her hands across her bosom
そして彼女は両手を胸の前で組んだ
and then she darted forward like a fish through the water
そして、水の中を魚のように飛び出しました
between the supple arms and fingers of the ugly polypi
醜いポリープのしなやかな腕と指の間
they were stretched out on each side of her
それらは彼女の両側に広がっていた
She saw that they all held something in their grasp
皆が何かを掴んでいるのが見えた
something they had seized with their numerous little arms
彼らは無数の小さな腕で何かを掴んだ
they were were white skeletons of human beings
それは人間の白い骸骨だった
sailors who had perished at sea in storms
嵐で海で亡くなった船員たち
and they had sunk down into the deep waters

そして、彼らは深い海に沈んでしまった
and there were skeletons of land animals
陸生動物の骨格もありました
and there were oars, rudders, and chests of ships
そして、オール、舵、船の箱がありました
There was even a little mermaid whom they had caught
捕まえた人魚姫もいました
the poor mermaid must have been strangled by the hands
哀れな人魚は両手で首を絞められていたに違いない
to her this seemed the most shocking of all
彼女にとって、これは最も衝撃的なことだった

finally, she came to a space of marshy ground in the woods
やがて、森の中の沼地にたどり着いた
here there were large fat water snakes rolling in the mire
ここには、泥沼で転がる大きな太った水蛇がいました
the snakes showed their ugly, drab-colored bodies
蛇は醜いくすんだ色の体を見せた
In the midst of this spot stood a house
その真ん中に一軒の家が建っていた
the house was built of the bones of shipwrecked human beings
家は難破した人間の骨で建てられました
and in the house sat the sea witch
そして、その家には海の魔女が座っていました
she was allowing a toad to eat from her mouth
彼女はヒキガエルに口から食べるのを許していた
just like when people feed a canary with pieces of sugar
ちょうど、カナリアに砂糖を飲ませる時のように
She called the ugly water snakes her little chickens
彼女は醜い水蛇を小さな鶏と呼んだ
and she allowed them to crawl all over her bosom
そして、胸のあちこちを這うのを許した

"I know what you want," said the sea witch
「あんたが何を望んでいるかはわかってるわ」と海の魔女は言いました

"It is very stupid of you to want such a thing"
「そんなものを欲しがるなんて、お前らの愚かなことだ」
"but you shall have your way, however stupid it is"
「しかし、どんなに愚かであろうと、あなたはあなたの道を歩むでしょう」
"though it will bring you to sorrow, my pretty princess"
「悲しみに暮れるだろうけど、可愛いお姫様」
"You want to get rid of your mermaid's tail"
「人魚の尻尾を消したい」
"and you want to have two supports instead"
「そして、代わりに2つのサポートが必要です」
"this will make you like the human beings on earth"
「そうすれば、あなたは地上の人間のようになるでしょう」
"and then the young prince might fall in love with you"
「そうすれば、若い王子様はあなたに恋をするかもしれません」
"and then you might have an immortal soul"
「そうすれば、あなたは不滅の魂を手に入れることができるかもしれません」
the witch laughed loud and disgustingly
魔女は大声で、うんざりしたように笑った
the toad and the snakes fell to the ground
ヒキガエルとヘビは地面に落ちました
and they lay there wriggling on the floor
そして、彼らは床にうごめきながら横たわっていた
"You are but just in time," said the witch
「あんたは間に合ったのよ」と魔女は言いました
"after sunrise tomorrow it would have been too late"
「明日の日の出からでは遅すぎただろう」
"I would not be able to help you till the end of another year"
「もう一年も経たないとお役に立てません」
"I will prepare a potion for you"
「ポーションを用意してあげる」
"swim up to the land tomorrow, before sunrise
「明日、日の出前に陸地まで泳いで行きなさい
"seat yourself there and drink the potion"
「そこに座ってポーションを飲んでください」

"after you drink it your tail will disappear"
「飲んだら尻尾が消える」
"and then you will have what men call legs"
「そうすれば、あなたは人間が脚と呼ぶものを手に入れるだろう」

"all will say you are the prettiest girl in the world"
誰もがあなたが世界で一番美しい女の子だと言うでしょう
"but for this you will have to endure great pain"
「しかし、そのためには、大きな苦痛に耐えなければならない」
"it will be as if a sword were passing through you"
「まるで剣があなたの中を通り抜けたかのようだ」
"You will still have the same gracefulness of movement"
「動きの優雅さは変わらない」
"it will be as if you are floating over the ground"
「まるで地面に浮かんでいるかのようだ」
"and no dancer will ever tread as lightly as you"
そして、あなたほど軽やかに歩くダンサーはいないでしょう
"but every step you take will cause you great pain"
「しかし、あなたが一歩踏み出すたびに、あなたは大きな痛みを伴います」
"it will be as if you were treading upon sharp knives"
「まるで鋭利なナイフを踏んでいるかのようだ」
"If you bear all this suffering, I will help you"
「あなたがこの苦しみに耐えられるなら、私はあなたを助けます」
the little mermaid thought of the prince
人魚姫は王子のことを考えました
and she thought of the happiness of an immortal soul
そして、彼女は不滅の魂の幸福を思い浮かべた
"Yes, I will," said the little princess
「ええ、そうします」と小さなお姫様は言いました
but, as you can imagine, her voice trembled with fear
しかし、ご想像の通り、彼女の声は恐怖で震えていました

"do not rush into this," said the witch
「急がないで」と魔女は言いました
"once you are shaped like a human, you can never return"
「一度人間の形になったら、もう二度と戻れない」
"and you will never again take the form of a mermaid"
そして、あなたは二度と人魚の姿をとることはありません
"You will never return through the water to your sisters"
「お前は二度と水を通って姉妹のところへは戻らない」
"nor will you ever go to your father's palace again"
「もう二度とお父さんの宮殿には行かない」
"you will have to win the love of the prince"
「王子様の愛を勝ち取らなければなりません」
"he must be willing to forget his father and mother for you"
「お父さんとお母さんを忘れて、あなたのために喜んでくれるに違いない」
"and he must love you with all of his soul"
「そして、彼は魂のすべてを尽くしてあなたを愛しているに違いありません」
"the priest must join your hands together"
「僧侶は手をつないでいなさい」
"and he must make you man and wife in holy matrimony"
「そして、神はあなたがたを聖なる結婚の男と妻としなければならない」
"only then will you have an immortal soul"
「そうして初めて、あなたは不滅の魂を手に入れることができる」
"but you must never allow him to marry another"
「しかし、あなたは彼が他の人と結婚することを許してはいけません」
"the morning after he marries another, your heart will break"
彼が別の人と結婚する翌朝、あなたの心は壊れるでしょう
"and you will become foam on the crest of the waves"
「そして、あなたは波の頂上で泡になる」
the little mermaid became as pale as death
人魚姆は死のように青ざめました
"I will do it," said the little mermaid
「やるよ」と人魚姫は言いました

"But I must be paid, also," said the witch
「でも、私もお金を払わなきゃいけないのよ」と魔女は言いました

"and it is not a trifle that I ask for"
「そして、それは私が求める些細なことではありません」

"You have the sweetest voice of any who dwell here"
「お前はここに住む者の中で一番甘い声の持ち主だ」

"you believe that you can charm the prince with your voice"
「あなたは自分の声で王子様を魅了できると信じています」

"But your beautiful voice you must give to me"
「しかし、あなたの美しい声は、あなたが私に与えなければなりません」

"The best thing you possess is the price of my potion"
「お前が持っている最高のものは、俺のポーションの値段だ」

"the potion must be mixed with my own blood"
「ポーションは自分の血と混ぜなければならない」

"only this makes it as sharp as a two-edged sword"
「これだけは両刃の剣のように鋭くなる」

the little mermaid tried to object to the cost
人魚姫はコストに異議を唱えようとしました

"But if you take away my voice..." said the little mermaid
「でも、私の声を奪ったら……」人魚姫は言いました

"if you take away my voice, what is left for me?"
「私の声を奪ったら、私には何が残る?」

"Your beautiful form," suggested the sea witch
「あなたの美しい姿よ」と海の魔女は言いました

"your graceful walk, and your expressive eyes"
「優雅な歩き方と表情豊かな瞳」

"Surely, wlth these you can enchain a man's heart?"
「まさか、これで人の心を縛ることができるのか?」

"Well, have you lost your courage?" the sea witch asked
「さて、勇気を失ったのかい?」と海の魔女は尋ねました

"Put out your little tongue, so that I can cut it off"
「お前の小さな舌を出して、俺が切り落とすように」

"then you shall have the powerful potion"

「そうすれば、強力なポーションを手に入れることができるだろう」
"It shall be," said the little mermaid
「そうなるよ」と人魚姫は言いました

Then the witch placed her caldron on the fire
それから魔女は大釜を火にかけました
"Cleanliness is a good thing," said the sea witch
「清潔さは良いことだ」と海の魔女は言いました
she scoured the vessels for the right snake
彼女は器をあさって正しい蛇を探した
all the snakes had been tied together in a large knot
すべての蛇は大きな結び目で結ばれていました
Then she pricked herself in the breast
それから彼女は自分の胸を刺した
and she let the black blood drop into the caldron
そして彼女は黒い血を大釜に落とした
The steam that rose twisted itself into horrible shapes
立ち上る湯気が恐ろしい形にねじれていった
no person could look at the shapes without fear
恐れずに形を見ることはできませんでした
Every moment the witch threw new ingredients into the vessel
魔女は一瞬一瞬、新しい材料を器に投げ入れた
finally, with everything inside, the caldron began to boil
最後に、すべてが中に入ると、大釜が沸騰し始めました
there was the sound like the weeping of a crocodile
ワニの泣き声のような音がした
and at last the magic potion was ready
そしてついに魔法の薬が出来上がりました
despite its ingredients, it looked like the clearest water
その成分にもかかわらず、それは最も澄んだ水のように見えました
"There it is, all for you," said the witch
「ほら、全部あなたのために」と魔女は言いました
and then she cut off the little mermaid's tongue
そして人魚姫の舌を切り落としました

so that the little mermaid could never again speak, nor sing
人魚姫が二度と話すことも歌うこともできないように
"the polypi might try and grab you on the way out"
「ポリープは途中であなたを捕まえようとするかもしれません」
"if they try, throw over them a few drops of the potion"
「もし彼らが試みるなら、ポーションを数滴投げてやれ」
"and their fingers will be torn into a thousand pieces"
「そして、彼らの指は千の裂け目となる」
But the little mermaid had no need to do this
しかし、人魚姫はそんなことをする必要はなかった
the polypi sprang back in terror when they saw her
ポリーピは彼女を見ると恐怖で跳ね返った
they saw she had lost her tongue to the sea witch
彼らは彼女が海の魔女に舌を失ったのを見ました
and they saw she was carrying the potion
そして、彼女がポーションを持っているのが見えました
the potion shone in her hand like a twinkling star
そのポーションは彼女の手の中できらめく星のように輝いていた

So she passed quickly through the wood and the marsh
それで娘は森と沼地を足早に通り抜けました
and she passed between the rushing whirlpools
そして彼女は急ぐ渦の間を通り過ぎた
soon she made it back to the palace of her father
やがて娘は父の宮殿に戻りました
all the torches in the ballroom were extinguished
舞踏室の松明は全て消えた
all within the palace must now be asleep
宮殿内の者は皆、眠りについたに違いない
But she did not go inside to see them
しかし、彼女は彼らを見るために中へは入らなかった
she knew she was going to leave them forever
彼女は永遠に彼らから離れることを知っていた
and she knew her heart would break if she saw them
そして、もし彼らを見たら心が折れてしまうことを知ってい

she went into the garden one last time
彼女は最後にもう一度庭に出た
and she took a flower from each one of her sisters
そして、姉妹の一人一人から花をもらいました
and then she rose up through the dark-blue waters
そして、紺碧の海を駆け上がった

the little mermaid arrived at the prince's palace
人魚姫は王子の宮殿に到着しました
the the sun had not yet risen from the sea
太陽はまだ海から昇っていなかった
and the moon shone clear and bright in the night
そして、月は夜に澄んで明るく輝いていました
the little mermaid sat at the beautiful marble steps
人魚姫は美しい大理石の階段に座っていました
and then the little mermaid drank the magic potion
そして、人魚姫は魔法の薬を飲みました
she felt the cut of a two-edged sword cut through her
彼女は両刃の剣が切り裂かれるのを感じた
and she fell into a swoon, and lay like one dead
そして彼女は気絶し、死んだように横たわった
the sun rose from the sea and shone over the land
太陽は海から昇り、陸を照らした
she recovered and felt the pain from the cut
彼女は回復し、切り傷の痛みを感じた
but before her stood the handsome young prince
しかし、彼女の前にはハンサムな若い王子が立っていました

He fixed his coal-black eyes upon the little mermaid
彼は石炭のように黒い瞳を人魚姫に向けました
he looked so earnestly that she cast down her eyes
彼は真剣なまなざしで見つめていたので、彼女は目を伏せた
and then she became aware that her fish's tail was gone
そして、魚の尻尾がなくなっていることに気づきました
she saw that she had the prettiest pair of white legs
彼女は自分がいちばんきれいな白い脚を持っているのを見ま

した
and she had tiny feet, as any little maiden would have
そして、小さな乙女がそうであるように、彼女は小さな足を持っていました
But, having come from the sea, she had no clothes
しかし、海から来たので、着るものがありませんでした
so she wrapped herself in her long, thick hair
それで、彼女は長くて太い髪に身を包みました
The prince asked her who she was and whence she came
王子は彼女に、自分は誰で、どこから来たのかと尋ねました
She looked at him mildly and sorrowfully
彼女は穏やかに、そして悲しげに彼を見た
but she had to answer with her deep blue eyes
しかし、彼女は深い青い瞳で答えなければならなかった
because the little mermaid could not speak anymore
人魚姫はもう話せなかったから
He took her by the hand and led her to the palace
王は娘の手を取り、宮殿に連れて行きました

Every step she took was as the witch had said it would be
彼女が踏み出した一歩一歩は、魔女が言った通りだった
she felt as if she were treading upon sharp knives
鋭利なナイフを踏んでいるような気がした
She bore the pain of the spell willingly, however
しかし、彼女はその呪文の痛みを喜んで耐えた
and she moved at the prince's side as lightly as a bubble
そして、王子のそばを泡のように軽やかに動かしました
all who saw her wondered at her graceful, swaying movements
彼女を見た者は皆、その優雅で揺れる動きに驚嘆した
She was very soon arrayed in costly robes of silk and muslin
彼女はすぐに絹とモスリンの高価なローブに身を包んだ
and she was the most beautiful creature in the palace
そして、彼女は宮殿で一番美しい生き物でした
but she appeared dumb, and could neither speak nor sing
しかし、彼女は口がきけず、話すことも歌うこともできませんでした

there were beautiful female slaves, dressed in silk and gold
そこには、絹と金の服を着た美しい女奴隷がいました
they stepped forward and sang in front of the royal family
彼らは前に出て、王室の前で歌った
each slave could sing better than the next one
各奴隷は、次の奴隷よりも上手に歌うことができました
and the prince clapped his hands and smiled at her
王子は手を叩いて彼女に微笑みかけました
This was a great sorrow to the little mermaid
これは人魚姫にとって大きな悲しみでした
she knew how much more sweetly she was able to sing
彼女は自分がどれだけ甘く歌うことができるかを知っていた
"if only he knew I have given away my voice to be with him!"
私が彼と一緒にいるために声を捧げたことを知っていたら!

there was music being played by an orchestra
オーケストラが奏でる音楽が流れていた
and the slaves performed some pretty, fairy-like dances
そして、奴隷たちは妖精のような可愛らしい踊りを披露しました
Then the little mermaid raised her lovely white arms
それから人魚姫は可愛らしい白い腕を上げました
she stood on the tips of her toes like a ballerina
彼女はバレリーナのようにつま先で立っていた
and she glided over the floor like a bird over water
そして彼女は水の上を飛ぶ鳥のように床の上を滑った
and she danced as no one yet had been able to dance
そして、まだ誰も踊れなかったように踊りました
At each moment her beauty was more revealed
その一瞬一瞬に、彼女の美しさはより明らかになっていった
most appealing of all, to the heart, were her expressive eyes
何よりも心を惹きつけたのは、彼女の表情豊かな瞳でした
Everyone was enchanted by her, especially the prince
誰もが、特に王子は彼女に魅了された
the prince called her his deaf little foundling

王子は彼女を耳の聞こえない小さなファウンドリングと呼んだ
and she happily continued to dance, to please the prince
そして、王子を喜ばせるために、喜んで踊り続けました
but we must remember the pain she endured for his pleasure
しかし、私たちは彼女が彼の喜びのために耐えた痛みを忘れてはなりません
every step on the floor felt as if she trod on sharp knives
床を一歩踏み出すたびに、鋭利なナイフを踏みつけたような感覚だった

The prince said she should remain with him always
王子は、いつも王子と一緒にいなさいと言いました
and she was given permission to sleep at his door
そして、彼女は彼の戸口で寝る許可を与えられました
they brought a velvet cushion for her to lie on
彼らは彼女が横になるためのベルベットのクッションを持ってきました
and the prince had a page's dress made for her
そして、王子は彼女のためにページのドレスを作ってもらいました
this way she could accompany him on horseback
そうすれば、彼女は馬に乗って彼に同行することができた
They rode together through the sweet-scented woods
二人は甘い香りのする森の中を一緒に走った
in the woods the green branches touched their shoulders
森の中では、緑の枝が二人の肩に触れていた
and the little birds sang among the fresh leaves
そして、小鳥たちは新鮮な葉の間を歌いました
She climbed with him to the tops of high mountains
彼女は彼と一緒に高い山の頂上に登りました
and although her tender feet bled, she only smiled
柔らかな足は血を流したが、彼女は微笑むだけだった
she followed him till the clouds were beneath them
彼女は雲が下に来るまで彼を追いかけた
like a flock of birds flying to distant lands

遥か彼方へ飛んでいく鳥の群れのように

when all were asleep she sat on the broad marble steps
みんなが眠りにつくと、娘は広い大理石の階段に座りました
it eased her burning feet to bathe them in the cold water
火照った足を和らげ、冷たい水に浸からせた
It was then that she thought of all those in the sea
その時、彼女は海にいるすべての人々のことを考えました
Once, during the night, her sisters came up, arm in arm
ある時、夜中に、姉妹たちが腕を組んでやって来ました
they sang sorrowfully as they floated on the water
二人は水面に浮かびながら悲しげに歌った
She beckoned to them, and they recognized her
彼女が手招きをすると、彼らは彼女に気づいた
they told her how they had grieved their youngest sister
彼らは、末の妹を悲しませたことを彼女に話しました
after that, they came to the same place every night
それ以来、彼らは毎晩同じ場所に来ました
Once she saw in the distance her old grandmother
ある時、彼女は遠くに年老いた祖母を見た
she had not been to the surface of the sea for many years
彼女はもう何年も海面に出ていなかった
and the old Sea King, her father, with his crown on his head
そして、頭に王冠をかぶった年老いた海王、彼女の父
he too came to where she could see him
彼もまた、彼女が彼を見ることができるところまで来ました
They stretched out their hands towards her
彼らは彼女に向かって手を伸ばした
but they did not venture as near the land as her sisters
しかし、彼女らは、姉妹のように陸地に近づかなかった

As the days passed she loved the prince more dearly
日が経つにつれて、彼女は王子を心から愛しました
and he loved her as one would love a little child
そして、彼は幼子を愛するように彼女を愛した
The thought never came to him to make her his wife
彼女を妻にしようという考えは彼には浮かばなかった

but, unless he married her, her wish would never come true
しかし、彼が彼女と結婚しない限り、彼女の願いは決して叶いません

unless he married her she could not receive an immortal soul
彼が彼女と結婚しない限り、彼女は不滅の魂を受け取ることができませんでした

and if he married another her dreams would shatter
そして、もし彼が別の人と結婚したら、彼女の夢は打ち砕かれるでしょう

on the morning after his marriage she would dissolve
彼の結婚の翌朝、彼女は解散した

and the little mermaid would become the foam of the sea
そして人魚姫は海の泡になるだろう

the prince took the little mermaid in his arms
王子は人魚姫を腕に抱きました

and he kissed her on her forehead
そして彼は彼女の額にキスをした

with her eyes she tried to ask him
彼女は目で彼に尋ねようとした

"Do you not love me the most of them all?"
「あなたがたは、わたしをいちばん愛してはいないのか」。

"Yes, you are dear to me," said the prince
「ええ、あなたは私にとって大切な人です」と王子は言いました

"because you have the best heart"
「最高の心を持っているから」

"and you are the most devoted to me"
「そして、あなたは私に最も献身的です」

"You are like a young maiden whom I once saw"
「お前はかつて見た乙女のようだ」

"but I shall never meet this young maiden again"
「でも、もう二度とこの若い娘には会えない」

"I was in a ship that was wrecked"
「難破した船に乗っていた」

"and the waves cast me ashore near a holy temple"
「そして、波は私を聖なる神殿の近くに岸に投げた」

"at the temple several young maidens performed the service"
「寺院では、何人かの若い乙女が礼拝を執り行いました」
"The youngest maiden found me on the shore"
「末っ子の乙女が岸辺で私を見つけた」
"and the youngest of the maidens saved my life"
「そして、乙女の末っ子が私の命を救ってくれた」
"I saw her but twice," he explained
「彼女に会ったのは2回だけだ」と彼は説明した
"and she is the only one in the world whom I could love"
「そして、彼女は私が愛せる世界で唯一の人です」
"But you are like her," he reassured the little mermaid
「でも、あんたもあの子と同じだよ」と彼は人魚姫を安心させました
"and you have almost driven her image from my mind"
「そして、あなたは私の心から彼女のイメージをほとんど追い払った」
"She belongs to the holy temple"
「彼女は聖なる神殿に属している」
"good fortune has sent you instead of her to me"
「幸運が彼女の代わりにあなたを私のもとに送った」
"We will never part," he comforted the little mermaid
「私たちは決して別れません」と彼は人魚姫を慰めました

but the little mermaid could not help but sigh
しかし、人魚姫はため息をつかずにはいられませんでした
"he knows not that it was I who saved his life"
「彼は、彼の命を救ったのが私だったことを知らない」
"I carried him over the sea to where the temple stands"
「私は彼を海を越えて神殿のあるところまで運びました」
"I sat beneath the foam till the human came to help him"
「人間が助けに来るまで、私は泡の下に座っていました」
"I saw the pretty maiden that he loves"
「彼が愛する可愛い乙女を見た」
"the pretty maiden that he loves more than me"
「私よりも愛する可愛い乙女」
The mermaid sighed deeply, but she could not weep
人魚は深いため息をつきましたが、泣くことができませんで

した
"He says the maiden belongs to the holy temple"
「乙女は聖なる神殿のものだそうです」
"therefore she will never return to the world"
「それゆえ、彼女は二度とこの世には戻ってこない」
"they will meet no more," the little mermaid hoped
「もう会わないよ」と人魚姫は願った
"I am by his side and see him every day"
「私は彼のそばにいて、毎日彼に会っています」
"I will take care of him, and love him"
「私は彼の世話をし、彼を愛する」
"and I will give up my life for his sake"
「彼のために命を捧げます」

Very soon it was said that the prince was to marry
まもなく、王子は結婚することになったと言われました
there was the beautiful daughter of a neighbouring king
隣の王様の美しい娘がいました
it was said that she would be his wife
彼女が彼の妻になると言われました
for the occasion a fine ship was being fitted out
この機会に、立派な船が艤装されていた
the prince said he intended only to visit the king
王子は、王様を訪ねるつもりだけだと言いました
they thought he was only going so as to meet the princess
王女に会いに行くだけだと思っていました
The little mermaid smiled and shook her head
人魚姫は微笑んで首を横に振った
She knew the prince's thoughts better than the others
彼女は王子の考えを他の誰よりもよく知っていた

"I must travel," he had said to her
「旅に行かなくちゃ」と彼は彼女に言った
"I must see this beautiful princess"
「この美しいお姫様に会わなきゃ」
"My parents want me to go and see her
「両親は彼女に会いに行ってほしいと言っています

"but they will not oblige me to bring her home as my bride"
「しかし、彼らは彼女を私の花嫁として家に連れて帰ることを私に義務付けません」
"you know that I cannot love her"
「私が彼女を愛せないことをあなたは知っています」
"because she is not like the beautiful maiden in the temple"
「だって、お寺の美女とは違うから」
"the beautiful maiden whom you resemble"
「お前に似た美しい乙女」
"If I were forced to choose a bride, I would choose you"
「花嫁を選ばせられるとしたら、あなたを選ぶ」
"my deaf foundling, with those expressive eyes"
「あの表情豊かな瞳の聾唖者」
Then he kissed her rosy mouth
それから彼は彼女のバラ色の口にキスをした
and he played with her long, waving hair
そして、彼は彼女の長い、波打つ髪で遊んだ
and he laid his head on her heart
そして彼は彼女の心臓に頭を置いた
she dreamed of human happiness and an immortal soul
彼女は人間の幸福と不滅の魂を夢見ていた

they stood on the deck of the noble ship
彼らは高貴な船の甲板に立っていた
"You are not afraid of the sea, are you?" he said
「海は怖くないんじゃないの?」と彼は言った
the ship was to carry them to the neighbouring country
船は彼らを隣国に運ぶことになっていた
Then he told her of storms and of calms
それから、嵐と静けさのことを彼女に話しました
he told her of strange fishes deep beneath the water
彼は彼女に、水面下の深いところに奇妙な魚がいることを話しました
and he told her of what the divers had seen there
そして、ダイバーたちがそこで見たものを彼女に話しました
She smiled at his descriptions, slightly amused
彼女は彼の説明に微笑み、少し面白がった

she knew better what wonders were at the bottom of the sea
彼女は海の底にどんな不思議があるのかをよく知っていた

the little mermaid sat on the deck at moonlight
人魚姫は月明かりの甲板に座っていた
all on board were asleep, except the man at the helm
舵を握る男を除いて、船上の全員が眠っていた
and she gazed down through the clear water
そして彼女は澄んだ水を見下ろした
She thought she could distinguish her father's castle
彼女は父の城を見分けることができると思った
and in the castle she could see her aged grandmother
そして城の中では、年老いたおばあさんの姿が見えました
Then her sisters came out of the waves
その時、姉妹たちが波から出てきた
and they gazed at their sister mournfully
そして悲しげに妹を見つめた
She beckoned to her sisters, and smiled
彼女は姉妹を手招きし、微笑んだ
she wanted to tell them how happy and well off she was
彼女は、自分がどれほど幸せで裕福であるかを彼らに伝えたかったのです
But the cabin boy approached and her sisters dived down
しかし、キャビンボーイが近づいてきて、姉妹は飛び降りました
he thought what he saw was the foam of the sea
彼は自分が見たのは海の泡だと思った

The next morning the ship got into the harbour
翌朝、船は港に入った
they had arrived in a beautiful coastal town
彼らは美しい海岸沿いの町に到着しました
on their arrival they were greeted by church bells
到着すると、教会の鐘が迎えてくれました
and from the high towers sounded a flourish of trumpets
高い塔からラッパの音が鳴り響いた
soldiers lined the roads through which they passed

兵士たちが通り過ぎる道に並んだ
Soldiers, with flying colors and glittering bayonets
派手な色ときらびやかな銃剣を持つ兵士たち
Every day that they were there there was a festival
彼らがそこにいる間、毎日お祭りがありました
balls and entertainments were organised for the event
舞踏会や催し物がイベントのために企画されました
But the princess had not yet made her appearance
しかし、王女はまだ姿を現していませんでした
she had been brought up and educated in a religious house
彼女は宗教的な家で育ち、教育を受けていました
she was learning every royal virtue of a princess
彼女は王女のあらゆる王室の美徳を学んでいた

At last, the princess made her royal appearance
ついに、王女は王室の姿を現しました
The little mermaid was anxious to see her
人魚姫は彼女に会いたがっていました
she had to know whether she really was beautiful
彼女は自分が本当に美しいかどうかを知る必要がありました
she was obliged to admit she really was beautiful
彼女は自分が本当に美しいことを認めざるを得なかった
she had never seen a more perfect vision of beauty
これほど完璧な美のビジョンを見たことはなかった
Her skin was delicately fair
彼女の肌は繊細に色白だった
and her laughing blue eyes shone with truth and purity
そして、彼女の笑う青い目は真実と純粋さで輝いていた
"It was you," said the prince
「お前だ」と王子は言いました
"you saved my life when I lay as if dead on the beach"
「浜辺で死んだように横たわっていたとき、あなたは私の命を救ってくれました」
"and he held his blushing bride in his arms"
「そして彼は顔を赤らめる花嫁を腕に抱いた」

"Oh, I am too happy!" said he to the little mermaid
「ああ、うれしすぎる!」と人魚姫に言いました
"my fondest hopes are now fulfilled"
「私の最大の願いが叶いました」
"You will rejoice at my happiness"
「あなたは私の幸せを喜ぶでしょう」
"because your devotion to me is great and sincere"
「あなたの私への献身は素晴らしく、誠実だからです」
The little mermaid kissed the prince's hand
人魚姫は王子の手にキスをしました
and she felt as if her heart were already broken
そして、彼女はすでに心が壊れているように感じました
His wedding morning would bring death to her
彼の結婚式の朝は彼女に死をもたらすだろう
she knew she was to become the foam of the sea
彼女は自分が海の泡になることを知っていた

the sound of the church bells rang through the town
教会の鐘の音が町中に響き渡った
the heralds rode through the town proclaiming the betrothal
伝令は婚約を宣言して町を通り抜けた
Perfumed oil was burned in silver lamps on every altar
芳香油は、すべての祭壇の銀のランプで燃やされました
The priests waved the censers over the couple
僧侶たちは香炉を振って二人に近づけた
and the bride and the bridegroom joined their hands
花嫁と花婿は手を合わせた
and they received the blessing of the bishop
そして、彼らは司教の祝福を受けた
The little mermaid was dressed in silk and gold
人魚姫は絹と金の服を着ていました
she held up the bride's dress, in great pain
彼女は花嫁のドレスを持ち上げ、ひどく苦しんだ
but her ears heard nothing of the festive music
しかし、彼女の耳には祝祭の音楽は何も聞こえなかった
and her eyes saw not the holy ceremony
彼女の目は聖なる儀式を見なかった

She thought of the night of death coming to her
彼女は死の夜がやってくることを考えた
and she mourned for all she had lost in the world
そして、この世で失ったすべてのものを嘆き悲しんだ

that evening the bride and bridegroom boarded the ship
その夜、花嫁と花婿は船に乗り込みました
the ship's cannons were roaring to celebrate the event
船の大砲が轟音を響かせて祝っていた
and all the flags of the kingdom were waving
王国の旗はみなびいていた
in the centre of the ship a tent had been erected
船の中央にはテントが張られていた
in the tent were the sleeping couches for the newlyweds
テントの中には、新婚夫婦のための寝台がありました
the winds were favourable for navigating the calm sea
風は穏やかな海を航行するのに好都合でした
and the ship glided as smoothly as the birds of the sky
そして、船は空の鳥のように滑らかに滑空しました

When it grew dark, a number of colored lamps were lighted
辺りが暗くなると、色とりどりのランプがいくつも灯された
the sailors and royal family danced merrily on the deck
船員と王室は甲板で陽気に踊った
The little mermaid could not help thinking of her birthday
人魚姫は自分の誕生日を思い出さずにはいられませんでした
the day that she rose out of the sea for the first time
彼女が初めて海から上がった日
similar joyful festivities were celebrated on that day
この日も同様の楽しいお祭りが祝われました
she thought about the wonder and hope she felt that day
彼女はあの日感じた驚きと希望に思いを馳せた
with those pleasant memories, she too joined in the dance
その楽しい思い出とともに、彼女もダンスに参加しました
on her paining feet, she poised herself in the air
痛む足で、彼女は宙に浮いた
the way a swallow poises itself when in pursued of prey

ツバメが獲物を追いかけているときの構え方
the sailors and the servants cheered her wonderingly
水夫や召使たちは不思議そうに彼女を喝采した
She had never danced so gracefully before
あんなに優雅に踊ったのは初めてだった
Her tender feet felt as if cut with sharp knives
彼女の柔らかな足は、鋭利なナイフで切られたかのようだった
but she cared little for the pain of her feet
しかし、彼女は足の痛みをほとんど気にかけなかった
there was a much sharper pain piercing her heart
心臓に鋭い痛みが走った
She knew this was the last evening she would ever see him
これが彼に会う最後の夜だとわかっていた
the prince for whom she had forsaken her kindred and home
彼女が親族と家を捨てた王子
She had given up her beautiful voice for him
彼女は彼のために美しい声をあきらめていた
and every day she had suffered unheard-of pain for him
そして毎日、彼女は彼のために前代未聞の苦痛に苦しんでいた
she suffered all this, while he knew nothing of her pain
彼女はこのすべてに苦しみましたが、彼は彼女の痛みについて何も知りませんでした
it was the last evening she would breath the same air as him
それは彼女が彼と同じ空気を吸う最後の夜だった
it was the last evening she would gaze on the same starry sky
同じ星空を眺める最後の夜だった
it was the last evening she would gaze into the deep sea
深海を眺める最後の夜だった
it was the last evening she would gaze into the eternal night
それは彼女が永遠の夜を見つめる最後の夜だった
an eternal night without thoughts or dreams awaited her
思考も夢もない永遠の夜が彼女を待っていた
She was born without a soul, and now she could never win one

彼女は魂を持たずに生まれ、今や魂を勝ち取ることはできなかった

All was joy and gaiety on the ship until long after midnight
真夜中を過ぎるまで、船の上では何もかもが喜びと陽気さに包まれていました
She smiled and danced with the others on the royal ship
彼女は微笑み、王室の船の上で他の者たちと踊った
but she danced while the thought of death was in her heart
しかし、彼女は死の思いが心に浮かんでいる間、踊った
she had to watch the prince dance with the princess
王子様がお姫様と踊るのを見なければならなかったのです
she had to watch when the prince kissed his beautiful bride
王子が美しい花嫁にキスをするのを見守らなければならなかった
she had to watch her play with the prince's raven hair
王子のカラスの髪で遊ぶのを見なければならなかった
and she had to watch them enter the tent, arm in arm
そして、彼女が腕を組んで天幕に入っていくのを見守らなければならなかった

after they had gone all became still on board the ship
彼らが去った後、全員が船上で静止した
only the pilot, who stood at the helm, was still awake
舵を握るパイロットだけが、まだ起きていた
The little mermaid leaned on the edge of the vessel
人魚姫は船の縁にもたれかかっていました
she looked towards the east for the first blush of morning
彼女は朝一番の顔を赤らめようと東の方を見た
the first ray of the dawn, which was to be her death
夜明けの最初の光線、それは彼女の死となるはずだった
from far away she saw her sisters rising out of the sea
遠くから、姉妹たちが海から上がってくるのが見えた
They were as pale with fear as she was
彼らは彼女と同じように恐怖で青ざめていた
but their beautiful hair no longer waved in the wind
しかし、その美しい髪はもはや風になびくことはなかった

"We have given our hair to the witch," said they
「髪の毛を魔女にあげたんだ」と二人は言いました
"so that you do not have to die tonight"
「今夜死ななくて済むように」
"for our hair we have obtained this knife"
「髪の毛のために、このナイフを手に入れました」
"Before the sun rises you must use this knife"
「太陽が昇る前に、このナイフを使わなければならない」
"you must plunge the knife into the heart of the prince"
「王子の心臓にナイフを突き刺さなければならない」
"the warm blood of the prince must fall upon your feet"
「王子の温かい血があなたの足に落ちるに違いない」
"and then your feet will grow together again"
「そうすれば、あなたの足は再び一緒に成長するでしょう」
"where you have legs you will have a fish's tail again"
「足があるところには、また魚の尻尾がある」
"and where you were human you will once more be a mermaid"
「そして、あなたが人間だったところで、あなたは再び人魚になるでしょう」
"then you can return to live with us, under the sea"
「じゃあ、海底に帰って一緒に暮らせばいい」
"and you will be given your three hundred years of a mermaid"
「そして、あなたは人魚の300年を与えられるでしょう」
"and only then will you be changed into the salty sea foam"
「そうして初めて、あなたは塩辛い海の泡に変わるのです」
"Haste, then; either he or you must die before sunrise"
「では、急いでください。彼かあなたか、どちらかが日の出前に死ななければならない」
"our old grandmother mourns for you day and night"
「私たちの年老いた祖母は、昼も夜もあなたのために嘆き悲しんでいます」
"her white hair is falling out"
「白い髪が抜け落ちている」
"just as our hair fell under the witch's scissors"
「私たちの髪の毛が魔女のハサミの下に落ちたように」

"Kill the prince, and come back," they begged her
「王子を殺して戻ってきてくれ」と彼らは彼女に懇願した
"Do you not see the first red streaks in the sky?"
「空に最初の赤い筋が見えませんか?」
"In a few minutes the sun will rise, and you will die"
「あと数分で太陽が昇り、お前は死ぬ」
having done their best, her sisters sighed deeply
最善を尽くした姉妹は、深いため息をついた
mournfully her sisters sank back beneath the waves
悲しげに妹たちは波の下に沈んでいった
and the little mermaid was left with the knife in her hands
そして人魚姫はナイフを手にしたまま残されました

she drew back the crimson curtain of the tent
彼女は天幕の真紅のカーテンを引いた
and in the tent she saw the beautiful bride
天幕の中で、美しい花嫁を見ました
her face was resting on the prince's breast
彼女の顔は王子の胸に寄りかかっていた
and then the little mermaid looked at the sky
そして人魚姫は空を見上げました
on the horizon the rosy dawn grew brighter and brighter
地平線上には、バラ色の夜明けがどんどん明るくなっていった
She glanced at the sharp knife in her hands
彼女は手に握られた鋭利なナイフをちらりと見た
and again she fixed her eyes on the prince
そして再び王子を見つめました
She bent down and kissed his noble brow
彼女は身をかがめ、彼の高貴な額にキスをした
he whispered the name of his bride in his dreams
彼は夢の中で花嫁の名前をささやいた
he was dreaming of the princess he had married
彼は自分が結婚した王女の夢を見ていた
the knife trembled in the hand of the little mermaid
人魚姫の手の中でナイフが震えた
but she flung the knife far into the waves

しかし、彼女はナイフを波の奥深くに投げつけた
where the knife fell the water turned red
ナイフが落ちたところで水が赤くなった
the drops that spurted up looked like blood
噴き上がった雫は血のようだった
She cast one last look upon the prince she loved
彼女は愛する王子に最後の視線を投げかけた
the sun pierced the sky with its golden arrows
太陽は黄金の矢で空を貫いた
and she threw herself from the ship into the sea
そして彼女は船から海に身を投げました
the little mermaid felt her body dissolving into foam
人魚姫は自分の体が泡に溶けていくのを感じました
and all that rose to the surface were bubbles of air
そして、水面に浮かび上がったのは空気の泡だけだった
the sun's warm rays fell upon the cold foam
太陽の温かい光が冷たい泡に降り注いだ
but she did not feel as if she were dying
しかし、彼女は自分が死ぬようには感じなかった
in a strange way she felt the warmth of the bright sun
不思議なことに、彼女は明るい太陽の暖かさを感じた
she saw hundreds of beautiful transparent creatures
彼女は何百もの美しい透明な生き物を見た
the creatures were floating all around her
生き物は彼女の周りに浮かんでいた
through them she could see the white sails of the ships
その向こうに船の白い帆が見えた
and through them she saw the red clouds in the sky
そして、その向こうに空に赤い雲が見えました
Their speech was melodious and childlike
彼らの話し方はメロディアスで子供っぽかった
but it could not be heard by mortal ears
しかし、それは人間の耳には聞こえなかった
nor could their bodies be seen by mortal eyes
また、彼らの体は人間の目には見えなかった
The little mermaid perceived that she was like them
人魚姫は、自分も彼らと同じだと感じました

and she felt that she was rising higher and higher
そして、彼女は自分がどんどん高く上がっていくのを感じました
"Where am I?" asked she, and her voice sounded ethereal
「ここはどこ?」と尋ねると、その声は幽玄に聞こえた
there is no earthly music that could imitate her
彼女を模倣できる地上の音楽はありません
"Among the daughters of the air," answered one of them
「空の娘たちだ」と一人が答えた
"A mermaid has not an immortal soul"
「人魚には不滅の魂はない」
"nor can mermaids obtain immortal souls"
「人魚は不滅の魂を手に入れることもできない」
"unless she wins the love of a human being"
「彼女が人間の愛を勝ち取らない限り」
"on the will of another hangs her eternal destiny"
「他人の意志に彼女の永遠の運命がぶら下がっている」
"like you, we do not have immortal souls either"
「お前みたいに、俺たちにも不滅の魂はない」
"but we can obtain an immortal soul by our deeds"
「しかし、私たちは自分の行いによって不滅の魂を手に入れることができます」
"We fly to warm countries and cool the sultry air"
「暖かい国に飛び、蒸し暑い空気を冷やす」
"the heat that destroys mankind with pestilence"
「疫病で人類を滅ぼす熱」
"We carry the perfume of the flowers"
「花の香りを運ぶ」
"and we spread health and restoration"
「健康と回復を広める」
"for three hundred years we travel the world like this"
「300年もの間、私たちはこうして世界を旅してきました」
"in that time we strive to do all the good in our power"
「その間、私たちは自分の力ですべての良いことをしようと努力します」
"when we succeed we receive an immortal soul"
「成功すると、不滅の魂がもらえる」

"and then we too take part in the happiness of mankind"
「そして、私たちも人類の幸福に加担するのです」
"You, poor little mermaid, have done your best"
「可哀想な人魚姫よ、よく頑張ったね」
"you have tried with your whole heart to do as we are doing"
「あなたがたは、私たちがやっているように、心を尽くしてやろうとした」
"You have suffered and endured an enormous pain"
「あなたは苦しみ、大きな痛みに耐えてきました」
"by your good deeds you raised yourself to the spirit world"
「あなたがたは、善行によって、霊界に引き上げられた」
"and now you will live alongside us for three hundred years"
そして今、あなたは300年間、私たちと共に生きるでしょう
"by striving like us, you may obtain an immortal soul"
「私たちのように努力することで、あなたは不滅の魂を手に入れることができます」
The little mermaid lifted her glorified eyes toward the sun
人魚姫は栄光の瞳を太陽に向けました
for the first time, she felt her eyes filling with tears
彼女は初めて、自分の目に涙があふれているのを感じた
On the ship she had left there was life and noise
彼女が去った船には、生命と騒音があった
she saw the prince and his beautiful bride searched for her
彼女は王子と彼の美しい花嫁が彼女を探しているのを見ました
Sorrowfully, they gazed at the pearly foam
悲しげに、彼らは真珠のような泡を見つめた
it was as if they knew she had thrown herself into the waves
まるで彼女が波に身を投げたことを知っているかのようだった
Unseen, she kissed the forehead of the bride
見えないところで、彼女は花嫁の額にキスをした
and then she rose with the other children of the air
そして、彼女は他の空の子らと一緒に立ち上がった
together they went to a rosy cloud that floated above
二人は一緒に、上空に浮かぶバラ色の雲のところへ行きました

"After three hundred years," one of them started explaining
「300年後だ」と一人が説明し始めた

"then we shall float into the kingdom of heaven," said she
「そうすれば、天の御国に浮かぶでしょう」と彼女は言いました

"And we may even get there sooner," whispered a companion
「もっと早く着くかも知れない」と仲間がささやいた

"Unseen we can enter the houses where there are children"
「見えないところで、子どものいる家に入ることができる」

"in some of the houses we find good children"
「良い子がいる家もある」

"these children are the joy of their parents"
「この子たちは親の喜び」

"and these children deserve the love of their parents"
「そして、これらの子供たちは両親の愛に値する」

"such children shorten the time of our probation"
「こういう子は保護観察期間を短くする」

"The child does not know when we fly through the room"
「子供は私たちが部屋を飛んでいくことを知りません」

"and they don't know that we smile with joy at their good conduct"
「そして、彼らは私たちが彼らの善行に喜びの笑みを浮かべていることを知りません」

"because then our judgement comes one day sooner"
「そうすれば、私たちの判断は1日早く来るから」

"But we see naughty and wicked children too"
「でも、いたずらっ子や意地悪な子も見かけます」

"when we see such children we shed tears of sorrow"
「そんな子どもたちを見ると、悲しみの涙を流す」

"and for every tear we shed a day is added to our time"
「そして、私たちが流す涙ごとに、一日が私たちの時間に加えられます」

The End / 最後です

www.tranzlaty.com

www.ingramcontent.com/pod-product-compliance
Lightning Source LLC
Chambersburg PA
CBHW011953090526
44591CB00020B/2759